THE STUDY
OF
ECCLESIASTICAL HISTORY

AN INAUGURAL LECTURE

GIVEN AT EMMANUEL COLLEGE, CAMBRIDGE

17 MAY 1945

BY

NORMAN SYKES

Dixie Professor of Ecclesiastical History

T0346169

CAMBRIDGE

AT THE UNIVERSITY PRESS

1945

CAMBRIDGE
UNIVERSITY PRESS

University Printing House, Cambridge CB2 8BS, United Kingdom

Published in the United States of America by Cambridge University Press, New York

Cambridge University Press is part of the University of Cambridge.

It furthers the University's mission by disseminating knowledge in the pursuit of education, learning and research at the highest international levels of excellence.

www.cambridge.org
Information on this title: www.cambridge.org/9781107634138

© Cambridge University Press 1945

First published 1945
Re-issued 2014

A catalogue record for this publication is available from the British Library

ISBN 978-1-107-63413-8 Paperback

THE STUDY OF
ECCLESIASTICAL HISTORY

'CHURCH HISTORY', observed the eccentric poly-
math William Warburton, 'making an important
part of our Theologic Studies, the Antiquarian
who delights to solace himself in the benighted days of
Monkish Owl-light sometimes passes for the Divine. But
while he flies from the sublime knowledge of Modern
Times, and yet never goes back far enough to seize the
pure and simple truths of primitive Christianity, he soon
betrays his adulterate species.' This depreciatory estimate
of the ecclesiastical historian, delivered with the pungency
of phrase peculiar to its author, is reminiscent of the famous
contrast in the fifteenth chapter of *The Decline and Fall
of the Roman Empire* between the theologian, who 'may
indulge the pleasing task of describing Religion as she
descended from heaven, arrayed in her native purity', and
the historian, who has the 'more melancholy duty' of dis-
covering 'the inevitable mixture of error and corruption
which she contracted in a long residence upon earth,
among a weak and degenerate race of beings'. Such
literary reflections may be thought perhaps to find an
academic counterpart in the tardy and comparatively

3

recent recognition of the status and importance of ecclesiastical history as measured by the foundation of professorships in that subject. Whereas the professors of divinity may trace their ancestry to the Lady Margaret or to that majestic lord who, in breaking the bonds of Rome, suffered a few doles from the financial profits to fall to the universities, and whilst the regius professorships of modern history enjoy the relatively respectable lineage of two centuries' continuance, the elevation of ecclesiastical history to equal dignity belongs in England to the academic reforms of the nineteenth century.

By an act of parliament of 1840 (3 & 4 Victoria, cap. 113) it was enacted that 'whereas her majesty has graciously intimated to parliament her royal will and intention to found two new professorships in the University of Oxford, and it is expedient that the same should be competently endowed...the two canonries in the said chapter of Christ Church (not being either of them a canonry annexed or to be annexed to any of the professorships already founded in the said university) which shall be thirdly and fourthly vacant, shall upon the vacancies thereof respectively, and the foundation of such professorships respectively, become and be permanently annexed and united thereto...and if either of such last-mentioned canonries be vacant before the foundation of such professorships, the same shall not be filled up until after such foundation'. In accordance with the royal intention, on 3 May 1842 a professorship of ecclesiastical history was founded and Mr Robert Hussey was appointed by the crown, the university providing an annual stipend of £300 until the appropriate canonry fell vacant, a circumstance (thanks to the gift of canonical longevity) not realised during the lifetime of the first professor. Here in Cambridge, by the munificence of Emmanuel College in devoting a large part of the benefaction which it enjoyed from Sir Wolstan Dixie to the needs of church history, there was established by a statute of 3 May 1882 'in the University a professorship to be called the Dixie Professorship of Ecclesiastical History'; and the vice-chancellor having declared the chair vacant on 18 April 1884, the first election in the following month brought Mandell Creighton to inaugurate its history. Meanwhile in King's College, London, the appointment on 23 December 1863 of Canon J. C. Robertson as Professor of Ecclesiastical History symbolised the emancipation of church history from the pseudonymous existence which it had enjoyed from 1844 to 1853 when F. D. Maurice, as Professor of Divinity, lectured on ecclesiastical history, and from the further period of a decade's probation when it was united in title with the chair of Old Testament and Hebrew. At Durham ecclesiastical history was associated with divinity in the canon-professorship annexed to that subject, from its establishment in 1833 until the conferment of the title of Professor of Church History on Dr Henry Gee in 1910; and upon his preferment to the deanery of Gloucester in 1918, the association was resumed until the creation of a separate Lightfoot Professorship of Divinity in 1943 brought Professor S. L. Greenslade to profess ecclesiastical history there.

The English student of church history may be pardoned therefore if he casts a half-envious eye upon the ordering of these matters according to the example of the best (and nearest) Reformed churches. For in North Britain after the Revolution of 1688 the restored Presbyterian church resolved to despoil its defeated rival, and William Carstares proposed to William III a short and easy way for the renovation of learning in the Scottish universities by the grant of £1200 sterling per annum out of the revenues of bishoprics falling to the crown by the act abolishing episcopacy in that country. As a special compliment to the new sovereign, Carstares designed to invite Dutch scholars to instruct his fellow-countrymen; and when the king decided to allow to each university the annual sum of £300 for the foundation of an additional professorship of divinity and ten bursaries in that subject, the special letter of donation to Edinburgh in 1694 declared his royal intention *dictis professoribus ab exteris per nos nostrisque successores vocandis et praestandis.* An unexplained hiatus occurred, however, between the provision of the endowment and the nomination of a professor; and when at length the first regius professor presented his credentials of appointment to the town council of Edinburgh on 10 November 1702, ten months after the accession of Queen Anne, he proved to be no Batavian divine but a native Scot, Mr John Cumming, and the title of his chair was that of ecclesiastical history. In 1707 the Third Mastership in St Mary's College, St Andrews, which had been frequently in abeyance, was revived and refounded by her

6

majesty as a professorship of ecclesiastical history, with emoluments obtained from the suppression of six exchequer bursaries founded by William III in 1693; and the new establishment was honoured by the translation of Professor Patrick Haldane, who had held the chair of Greek at St Salvator's College. Thus did Scotland enjoy its own version of Queen Anne's bounty; and that queen, although her heart was, as she confessed, 'entirely English' and her especial devotion 'to the interests and religion of the Church of England', became accountable in some wise also as the Church of Scotland's glory.

At Glasgow the foundation of a professorship of ecclesiastical history was the outcome of another change of dynasty and consequentially of the loyalty shewn to George I during the Jacobite rebellion of 1715 by that university, and especially by the faculty of theology; in return for which they represented to the king the need of an endowment for this chair and of an augmentation of the stipends of the professorships of law and medicine founded out of the bounties of William III and of Anne. Accordingly, on 4 July 1716, his majesty, taking notice that *adhuc deest provisio Professori Historiae Ecclesiasticae*, and in order that *dicta Universitas et ecclesiae et statui magis utile reddatur*, gave £100 sterling per annum out of the revenues of the archbishopric of Glasgow *tanquam perpetuum sallarium Professori Historiae Ecclesiasticae in dicta Universitate*. In fulfilment of the foundation, on 13 January 1720 George I nominated Mr James Dick, minister of the gospel in the parish of Carluke, to the professorship;

but on 15 March following, a majority resolution of the university to ask the presbytery of Lanark to release the professor-designate from his parochial charge was resisted by a dissentient minority, which carried its opposition to the general assembly and there secured a refusal to grant the release. Since therefore, as the official academic record recites, 'some difficulties had intervened which had obstructed the settling a fit and qualified person in the office of professor of church history in the said university', the crown obligingly made a second nomination, of Mr William Anderson, who was admitted by the university on 29 August 1721 as its first Professor of Ecclesiastical History. At Aberdeen the royal commission of inquiry into the state of the universities of Scotland recommended in 1831 the supplying of a deficiency by the establishment of a professorship of church history; and on 18 June 1833 Principal Dewar of Marischal College became also Professor of Ecclesiastical History, whilst at King's College on 30 December 1843 Professor W. Robinson Pirie became Professor of Church History, and on the union of the two colleges in 1860 continued as sole professor of this subject in the university.

The fair promise offered by the early planting of professorships of ecclesiastical history in three of the four Scottish universities was destined soon to disappointment. For ecclesiastical human nature, even Scottish ecclesiastical human nature, is not exempt from the infirmity and frailties of its temporal counterpart; and it is perhaps with less surprise than sorrow that the English student learns that within thirty years of the first appointment to the new professorship at Edinburgh, it was reported of the third holder of the office, Matthew Craufurd (1721–36), that 'he has £100 and really does nothing for it. He will give no private colleges but for money, and nobody comes to him. His public praelections are not frequented; he will not have six or seven hearers.' His successor Patrick Cumming (1737–62) lectured for only one hour per week for four months of the year; and when he made over the chair to his son, Robert Cumming (1762–88), the latter improved even on this neglect, being said never to have delivered any lectures, thus converting the office into a sinecure. At Glasgow a royal commission gave new statutes to the university on 19 September 1727, by which the professors of divinity, law, medicine, oriental languages, and church history were required to teach their respective subjects whenever five students applied to them, and to 'give not under four lessons every week'. Notwithstanding which explicit order, the second Professor of Ecclesiastical History, William Rouet (1752–85), first reduced the duties to two hours' lecturing per week, and during the greater part of his tenure ceased to lecture altogether. The story is one of loss as well as of gain. Indeed, Dr David Welsh, who was appointed to the regius chair at Edinburgh in 1831, permitted himself the strongest expression of his conviction that 'the way in which the duties of the chair...had been discharged in the different universities for a century past (from mistaken views of the nature of the subject) was such that in many instances the existence of the subject had proved an evil to the church'.

'*Tis Sixty Years Since* was the second title of Scott's first novel of the Waverley series; and although it is only sixty-one years to-day since the election of Mandell Creighton as the first Dixie Professor of Ecclesiastical History, the renown conferred upon the chair and its subject by the distinction and work of the three holders whose tenure spans the interval between 1884 and to-day may be held justly to counterbalance the comparative brevity of its history. Of the first two professors, Creighton and Gwatkin, it is a truism to say that they being dead, yet speak to continuing generations of students of church history, to whom their works are an indispensable part of the equipment of their study. Moreover, the recollection of their methods and influence has been preserved by pupils and friends, in the case of Creighton by Figgis, and in that of Gwatkin by Professor Whitney in his inaugural lecture and more recently by the Professor of Medieval History upon a similar occasion. I should count it a happy circumstance for myself had I been able to speak of Professor James Pounder Whitney from like personal knowledge. But the privilege of personal intimacy was denied to me. I met him on only two occasions and corresponded with him hardly more frequently. Fortunately there are not lacking those able to speak of his inspiration to pupils and of his services in the editorial direction of the *Cambridge Medieval History*, as more generally of the influence which he possessed here; and it would be an impertinence on my part to attempt to add anything to what has been said by Mr R. E. Balfour in the memoir prefixed to the posthumous revision of Whitney's *History of the Reformation*, and in the recent inaugural lecture of the Professor of Medieval History. But even to one who knew Whitney only *ab extra* through the medium of his writings there may be allowed a brief expression of the debt which he, together with all students of ecclesiastical history, owes to his work.

Perhaps the first thing which strikes the reader of Whitney's works is the catholicity of his learning. Mr Balfour has recorded his observation that 'he had lectured on every period but one of ecclesiastical history', and the bibliography of his writings appended to Mr Balfour's memoir illustrates the range and width of his interests. This catholicity of knowledge inspired and supported his conviction of the fundamental unity of church history, even through such periods as the Reformation where at first sight disunion seems writ large on the face of its record, but where, as his essay on *Continuity throughout the Reformation* proves, he was able to bring cogent evidence in substantiation of his contention. This same conviction led to his emphatic iteration of the importance of the episcopate as the external symbol and providential agent of this underlying unity of the church, which was the theme of his Hulsean Lectures. A typical illustration of the range of his learning may be found in the magisterial survey of the development of papal power from Gregory the Great to the Conciliar Movement in the essay on *The Medieval Church in the West* which he contributed to *Our Place in Christendom*. Within this wide framework, Whitney had his favourites, of course; he was an acknowledged master of the epoch of the Hildebrandine reforms, reinterpreting the work of Hildebrand in the light of fresh evidence and of the work of foreign scholars; and his interest in and authoritative surveys of the Reformation were continuous throughout the entire span of his long life of historical study and writing. But knowledge of a particular period in great detail on the one hand never caused him to lose sight of its salient features, as the illuminating, synoptic survey of the varied currents of the age in his essay already mentioned on *Continuity throughout the Reformation* abundantly shews. On the other hand, the reader of his chapter on *The Conversion of the Teutons* in the *Cambridge Medieval History* might pardonably conclude from its detailed scholarship that this period represented his specialist study. Or if a characteristic example be sought of the exactness of his research, it may be found in the information first mentioned in a modest footnote to his Church Congress paper on *The National Church and the Papacy* (and later referred to also in a footnote to his essay on *The Growth of Papal Jurisdiction before Nicholas I*) that he had verified for himself the calculation of a previous writer that between 688 and 1050 there were consecrated 376 English bishops, and in no single case is there any sign of a papal share either in appointment or consecration.

Next to this catholicity of learning the reader of Whitney's works is struck by his ubiquitous familiarity with the great secondary writers of past times on church history. In his inaugural lecture he had laid especial stress on this necessary qualification, marking its presence in Creighton and Gwatkin, and warning against the danger of its neglect in the vogue of research into manuscript sources. His practice fully confirmed his precept; and his careful habit of adding to references to standard secondary authorities in footnotes a few critical comments upon particular points of importance in them is of invaluable service to readers, directing them to authorities which might otherwise be missed and suggesting fruitful lines of investigation. In his extensive knowledge of the contribution made by previous workers in the field of church history Whitney followed the example of the Caroline divines, whose ambition to be acquainted with whatsoever had been written aforetime for their learning he so much admired. In all his writings he had the needs of others in mind; and this concern for other, and especially for younger, students found particular expression in the series of *Texts for Students* and of *Helps for Students of History*, in the editorship of which he bore a leading part; and which aimed to provide in the former case cheap editions of some of the principal authorities for the study of church history and in the second manuals to guide the steps of the student about to embark on unfamiliar fields. Since both series appeared at the time of my undergraduate days I can speak from personal knowledge of their value, and I could wish that they might be made available for the post-war generation of students. The consummation of this devotion to the service of students was his final bequest of his rich library, which now from the shelves of the Seeley Historical Library invites us to remember his work by carrying on his traditions.

To myself, upon whose shoulders there rests now the responsibility of attempting to stand in the succession to so great a heritage, the contemplation of its history brings a humbleness and sense of evident inadequacy. *Quis idoneus?* One thing perhaps I may make bold to plead to commend myself to your indulgence. Thanks to the circumstance, shared with Whitney, of having been born and bred up in the West Riding of Yorkshire, I had the good fortune to come in my 'teens under the influence of three Cambridge scholars. From Professor A. J. Grant I first learnt an enthusiasm for historical studies and an example of both the teaching and writing of history, the memory of which stirs gratefully within me now. To Dr Neville Figgis I owe my first stimulus to the study of church history and the encouragement to read widely in its velvet study, combined with the conviction that in the history of the Christian church the interpretation of the purpose of human history and of individual destiny is made plain. When I began to approach the more technical problems of its study, I received from Dr W. H. Frere my first introduction to the nature and contents of an episcopal register, with advice about other sources to be consulted. This combined influence constitutes a threefold cord not easily to be broken. At a later time in Oxford I learnt from Sir Charles Firth the more specialised technique of historical research, alike from the example of his own exact and austere scholarship and by the friendly yet forceful criticism to which he submitted my amateur efforts; and not least to the prodigal generosity of his friendship do I owe a standard to which I hope I may never be unfaithful in aspiration, however far I may fall short in execution. At the same time Dr E. W. Watson set my feet firmly in the paths which I have ever since tried to follow by admitting me to so much as I could understand of his oecumenical learning in church history, and by suggesting a variety of lines of reading for future study. From his conversation I recollect *obiter dicta* which set in new perspective periods, persons, and movements; and to his continuing friendship I owe the encouragement to persevere. To his constant help and kindness I am indebted for whatsoever claims I may have to stand here to-day as a teacher and student of church history. Being transplanted next by Sir Ernest Barker to King's College, London, I began there that relationship so aptly described by Whitney as one of 'pupil disguised as colleague' with Professor Claude Jenkins, from which for twenty years I have drawn such generous draughts of time and counsel as he is wont to give to younger brethren. To the oecumenicity of knowledge possessed by these my teachers in church history I cannot pretend; but this at least I can affirm, that under the inspiration of their influence I have sought, so far as the exigencies of teaching have allowed, to draw all my cares and studies that way, so that from the first kindling of an enthusiasm for ecclesiastical history more than thirty years ago by the encouragement of three Cambridge scholars, I come now once more to Cambridge to learn and receive. If in addition to what I hope to learn, I am enabled to give some help and encouragement, such as I have myself so liberally received, to other students to set aside, so far as in them lies, all other cares and studies, I shall account myself not to have laboured wholly in vain.

In the painful yet salutary process of self-examination upon which I have been engaged in prospect of the privilege of working here, I need hardly say that two things have fortified my resolution; the warmth of friendship which I have received on all sides, and the especial good fortune of the Dixie professor in that provident kindness of Emmanuel College which has ensured him from the outset a home in its society. As a student of church history I am not unaware of the unenviable situation of *episcopi vagantes* and of the evils which they have brought upon the church; nor of the abhorrence in which St Benedict held the *monachorum...genus gyrovagum*; and I rejoice the more therefore to be delivered from the perilous position of a *professor vagans* by the *stabilitas* given to me through membership of this College. I come moreover from the fourteenth-century College of Robert de Eglesfield, founded in order that *per viros in theologia provectos fides catholica roboratur, universalis ecclesia decoratur, christianis populus quietatur, et verbo instructionis evangelice salubriter informatur*; and I come to the sixteenth-century College of Sir Walter Mildmay, founded 'to render as many as possible fit for the administration of the Divine Word and Sacraments; and that from this seed-ground the English church might have those that she can summon to instruct the people and undertake the office of pastors, which is a thing necessary above all others'; and to enable both Fellows and Scholars to devote themselves to Sacred Theology. The differences of time and of attendant phraseology hardly veil a fundamental similarity of intention and spirit. And where could a student of church history feel more at home than in the College which within a generation of its foundation sent forth from the number of its Fellows two of the four English representatives to the Synod of Dort, Joseph Hall and Samuel Ward, there to participate in the affirmation of an apparently triumphant Calvinism; which within another generation nourished among its society some of the most eminent of the Cambridge Platonists, Benjamin Whichcote, Ralph Cudworth, Nathaniel Culverwell and John Smith, whose studies in that theology called by Eglesfield *arbor deifica tam fructifera* were for the healing of the controversies of a fiercely disputatious age, and whose principles marked the decline of the system of Calvin's *Institutes*; which after the restoration of crown and church called to its Mastership one of the most famous of its sons, William Sancroft, the pattern of Caroline high-churchmanship, who, notwithstanding, in his primacy, as Dr Jenkins has observed, 'shewed greater friendship to members of the foreign Reformed churches than perhaps any other archbishop of Canterbury'; and which in the Georgian age nurtured William Law, whose devotional writings influenced his greater contemporary John Wesley and in after times also John Keble, watering therein the fields of evangelical and tractarian piety, whilst his polemical divinity in the *Three Letters to the Bishop of Bangor* supplied a defence of the high Anglican doctrine of a hierarchical church against Hoadly's conception of a purely invisible society, and constituted a link thereby between the later Caroline divines and the men of the Oxford Movement? Whether planted or transplanted into such a College, the student of ecclesiastical history may say *Laetus sorte mea*, for the lines are fallen indeed to him in a fair ground.

If I were asked to specify what seemed to me the most significant development in historical studies during the twenty years between Whitney's assumption of the office of Dixie professor at the end of the first world-war and his laying it down on the eve of the second, I should point to the expansion and vogue of research. This period witnessed to a considerable degree the fulfilment of Bury's vision expounded in his inaugural lecture, of the advance of historical study as consisting largely of 'the gathering of materials bearing upon minute local events, the collation of MSS and the registry of their small variations, the patient drudgery in archives of states and municipalities, all the microscopic research that is carried on by armies of toiling students'. The evidence of this labour was ubiquitous and surrounded us on every side, in the volume of erudite monographs published year by year, in the multiplication of articles in learned periodicals, in students seeking to qualify for research degrees whose name was legion, and even in the dangerous invasion of undergraduate courses by somewhat premature specialisation. To myself the symbol and focus of this vogue, as seen from the vantage point of a teacher of the University of London, was the Institute of Historical Research, which not only provided invaluable technical facilities for learning the craft of research, but also performed an even more vital function in my judgment by bringing together into a truly co-operative society both teachers and pupils and helping thereby to overcome the barriers created by specialised study. The positive contribution of this devotion to research to historical study is evident and needs no iteration. But the tendency was not unattended by dangers. Professor Whitney, in his inaugural lecture, and the Professor of Medieval History on a like recent occasion called attention to the dangers of neglect of printed authorities in the zeal for discovery of manuscript sources, and of a consequent decline in familiarity with the classics of historical writing. Furthermore the peril of over-specialisation is no less real both to teacher and pupil, and the barriers erected by an undue restriction of interest constitute an obstacle also to the good estate of historical studies.

Ecclesiastical history, together with other branches of historical study, has shared in the benefits of this devotion to research. If the Professor of Medieval History has justly claimed the previous Dixie professors as predecessors of his own chair, the harvest of their sowing has been richly garnered in the contribution made to the ecclesiastical history of the Middle Ages by Cambridge scholars, which it would be as invidious as impertinent to particularise. In this field the specialist studies of the last twenty years have yielded a large return, and the promise of the future is contained in Professor Brooke's avowal that 'from the nature of his subject every medievalist must be in some degree an ecclesiastical historian'. Nor is there any reason to doubt, from the literary activity of this period, that the history of the early centuries of the Christian church will continue to exercise its perennial appeal to students, not least in the university which cherishes the memory and traditions of Lightfoot and Gwatkin. In the modern centuries perhaps the ground has been less densely populated by researchers, partly no doubt because the historian of post-Reformation Europe has more justification for absolving himself from the onerous obligation to investigate the differing confessional statements and systems of church order which have issued from the break-up of the ecclesiastical unity of the medieval *Respublica Christiana*. But in all periods church history has been enriched by historical research; and the problem of the harmonious relationship between specialised studies and more general surveys of wider epochs presses with particular gravity within the sphere of its interest.

The Dixie professor is Professor of Ecclesiastical History without subdivision; and traditionally the scope of professors of church history has been almost without limit. In the Scottish foundations of the eighteenth century their province embraced the whole period at least from Abraham to the Reformation. The royal commissioners of enquiry into the state of the universities of Scotland, appointed in 1826, cross-examined the professors of ecclesiastical history narrowly in regard to this particular point. Professor Meiklejohn, who had held the chair at Edinburgh for nearly thirty years, upon being asked 'how far have you actually brought down your account of the history of the church?' replied: 'To the Mahometan Impostor. I have hardly exhausted what precedes, and I find it takes more than three years to get through it', though he lectured five hours each week. His brother of St Andrews, Professor Buist, who lectured only two hours per week, 'had not yet been able to descend below the fourteenth century'; whilst Professor McTurk at Glasgow, lecturing two hours per week through three sessions, divided his course into three sections; first 'the history of revealed religion under the Old Testament dispensation with an account of the civil and political institutions of the Hebrews', secondly 'the history of the Christian church from the birth of our Saviour to the present times with an account of the state of society and learning during all that period', and thirdly the 'history of the Church of Scotland until the Reformation' combined with the history of the Reformation in Germany and other countries of Europe. The commissioners sought a solution of the problem not by abbreviating the scope of the subject but by increasing the number of lectures where necessary. Recommending a course of five hours each week (of which four should be lectures and one for exercises), extending over two academic sessions, they advised that the first year should embrace 'a historical view of the Old Testament dispensation, the introduction of Christianity, the apostolic age, and a historical and critical account of the apostolic fathers'; and that the second series should cover the 'history of the dissemination and establishment of Christianity, of the opinions which have been entertained as to its doctrines and morality, and of the various forms under which it has been administered; and the polity, laws, and government of the Church of Scotland'. Professor James Robertson, on succeeding to the Edinburgh chair in 1844, attempted to carry out this ambitious scheme with the important modification that during three sessions instead of two, 'he went over the ages of church history from the dim old days of Abraham down to those of Luther'. Even this was not sufficient, and later he extended his course to four sessions so that he might give 'a full and minute history of all the outward and inward experience of the church from the times of Abraham'. There is little wonder that he worked in his study until past midnight and resumed his labour at 4 a.m., and that he died at the age of fifty-seven. It was in conformity with this conviction of the importance of the Old Testament that the second regius professor at Oxford, A. P. Stanley, insisted on beginning with the call of Abraham. 'From this point we shall start, and from this shall be prepared to enter on the history of the people of Israel as the true beginning and prototype of the Christian church. So in old times it was ever held.... So it must be in the nature of the case.' And Gwatkin declined 'to find fault' with this programme, whilst refusing to imitate it. By general consent, however, the Old Testament dispensation shortly disappeared from the responsibility of the professors of church history; and when a chair of ecclesiastical history was established in Trinity College, Dublin, in 1850 by the munificence of the Lord Primate of Ireland, the first professor, Samuel Butcher, in his inaugural lecture defined his ambition 'to go over the whole period from the foundation of the Church to the present time once every two years'. Even this limitation of territory leaves the field of the professor of ecclesiastical history difficult to envisage and to execute.

For myself I have to confess that I cannot think that abandonment of the width of interest associated with the study of ecclesiastical history would be justifiable. Some limitations are imposed by the practical exigencies of teaching and writing. But the range of sympathy and interest must remain. It is demanded by the nature of the subject. For the church historian is concerned with nothing other or less than Christ's holy, catholic church, that is the whole congregation of Christian people dispersed throughout the whole world; and dispersed also through nearly twenty centuries of history, yet with a vital consciousness of the unity and continuity of its tradition. The range of the ecclesiastical historian must extend therefore from 'the pure and simple truths of primitive Christianity' to 'the sublime knowledge of modern times'. Tradition is here a sound guide. For Gwatkin, after avowing that in the work of teaching he would content himself mainly with 'the twelve centuries or so from the destruction of Jerusalem to the culmination of the papal power', added, almost in the same breath, 'yet for my own sake I shall have to keep an eye on the whole range of history from first to last'. So also Whitney, after observing that every student of church history should be at home in the early centuries of its development, proceeded to affirm that he would not 'lose his interest in medieval times or in the many dramas of the Reformation', whilst emphasising the need of increased attention to the nineteenth century. Consonant with this standpoint is the expectation of candidates offering the church history section in Part II of the Theological Tripos that they should shew a general knowledge of the development of the church from the apostolic age to modern times, combined with more detailed study of a special period. I hope I may not be thought too bold a trespasser, as I certainly may not be accused of innovation, if I confess the aspiration to lecture on subjects, general or specialised, of the medieval period, and if occasion offers, to venture in the field of early church history with particular relation to the origins and growth of the Christian ministry, and at the same time to devote chief attention to the epoch of the Reformation and the working out of its diverse issues in succeeding centuries, especially the last two centuries.

Similarly the traditions of the Dixie professorship encourage me to attempt, side by side with the wider survey incumbent upon a teacher, the work of more detailed research into a particular subject. From Sir Charles Firth I learned that such concentration need not and should not lead to a narrowing of interest or knowledge. My own experience of a decade's investigation of the life and times of archbishop Wake has confirmed this judgment. For Wake's *English Version of the Genuine Epistles of the Apostolic Fathers* leads the reader backwards to the age in which they wrote and forward to the definitive edition of their works by Lightfoot. From Wake's preoccupation with the Convocation controversy of his own day the way runs backwards to the medieval origins and history of English Provincial Synods and forward to their revival in the last century. By his important correspondence with the Gallican divines and his friendship to Père Le Courayer's investigations of Anglican Orders, the student is carried back to the early centuries of ecclesiastical development and in particular to the growth of the papacy, and forward thence to the Anglican Reformation and even to the Conversations at Malines. Through Wake's extensive correspondence and dealings with the Lutheran and Reformed churches of the continent a link is established between the relations of the Church of England and foreign Protestants in the sixteenth and seventeenth centuries and the oecumenical movements of the present time. In such a study frontiers alike of time and place dissolve, and the history of the universal church becomes mirrored and reflected in that of a particular theme and epoch. Such a dream, if I may borrow some words of Gwatkin, 'will give a fair amount of room even for such a glutton for work as your ideal professor ought to be'; and even though its realisation will probably prove beyond the compass of its dreamer, at least the avowal of it as an ideal may serve as a goad to spur me on to as near approximation as may be possible.

But howsoever busy a professor may be, he ought not to live and work *in vacuo*. The good estate of his subject demands students as well as sources. Whence may the teacher of ecclesiastical history look for the recruitment of collaborators and helpers? Primarily to students reading the Historical and Theological Triposes. Speaking in the university before which Acton in his inaugural lecture affirmed his conviction that 'the first of human concerns is religion, and it is the salient feature of the modern centuries', and Creighton on similar occasion asserted the primacy of ecclesiastical history as a guide to the understanding of European history as a whole, no word of mine could add emphasis or authority to their statement of the importance of a knowledge of church history to the historical student. But perhaps I may be permitted the expression of a personal hope that, when with the return of peace the Historical Tripos is restored to its former completeness, there may be a period of modern church history among the Special Subjects for Part II, whether by the revival of that on the Elizabethan Church or by the substitution of another. In the Theological Tripos church history has its recognised place, especially in the Section of Part II devoted to its study. In both these connections the difficulty of procuring suitable editions of standard texts and sources, to which Whitney drew attention in his inaugural lecture, is likely to be more formidable at the end of the second world-war than twenty-five years ago, as has been recently emphasised by the Professor of Medieval History. Notwithstanding, it is my hope that through both the Historical and Theological Triposes many students may be drawn to devote themselves to further study of ecclesiastical history; and the value of the Lightfoot Scholarship in providing means for the fulfilment of such ambition is abundantly proved by the list of holders who during their tenure have laid the foundations of a later distinction in this field.

More particularly if, as Professor Powicke has observed, 'from one point of view the Christian religion is a daily invitation to the study of history', church history should form an essential constituent of the education of the Christian ministry. From the early centuries of its story flow the streams which irrigate all Christian societies, of the medieval church and of its ambitious endeavour to create a *Respublica Christiana* we are all heirs, to the drama of the Reformation epoch the Protestant churches and the Roman church of the counter-Reformation alike

27

owe their continuing *differentiae*, and from the great missionary expansion of the nineteenth century arise the problems and present impulse towards reunion of the churches. A quarter of a century ago Whitney, in his inaugural lecture, rejoiced at the inclusion of the nineteenth century in the periods of church history studied; and the recent comprehensive *History of the Expansion of Christianity* of Professor Latourette has emphasised the importance of the last century in the *Weltanschauung* of the Christian historian. I welcome cordially the possibility that this theme may find a more prominent place in both the Historical and Theological Triposes. Yet in the field of theological study, church history has to contend for due recognition against vociferous competitors. I remember when, twenty-five years ago, I was reading with Canon Streeter for the Honour School of Theology, he regarded church history as a dull subject fit only for second-rate men (a heresy which he handsomely recanted later in his introduction to *The Primitive Church*), and did his utmost to persuade me to offer instead a special subject in the philosophy of religion. To-day perhaps the dominant claims proceed from an aggressively dogmatic theological system, which is apt to shew impatience of both the slow processes and modest results of the historical method. Yet disciples of a historical religion may not forget that the historical method is proper to their studies; and we shall do well to recall the words of Lightfoot in his excursus on *The Christian Ministry*, applicable to-day to that as to other fields of theological enquiry, that 'in this clamour of antagonistic opinions history is obviously the sole, upright, impartial referee; and the historical mode of treatment will therefore be strictly adhered to in the following investigation. The doctrine in this instance at all events is involved in the history.' In the end, moreover, the student of ecclesiastical history enjoys the consolation that to his lot falls the recording or the reading of the decline and fall of successive theological systems, triumphant and dominant in their turn, yet in the providence of God having their day and ceasing to be.

But if in some respects the contemporary vogue in theological study is not wholly favourable to the historical method, the prevalent intellectual climate in historical studies seems unusually congenial to the peculiar contribution which in my judgment ecclesiastical history may offer to the discipline of historical thinking. Perhaps the change, which within a generation has taken place in the conceptions entertained by historians of the nature of their subject, is best measured by a comparison of Bury's inaugural lecture delivered in 1903 with Mr Balfour's essay on History in the *Cambridge University Studies* published in 1933. From the standpoint of philosophy also Professor R. G. Collingwood's sketch of his mature view of history, in his British Academy lecture on *Human Nature and Human History* in 1936, may well cause historians on a long view bitterly to regret the turning aside of his last days under the pressure of present events from his projected work on *The Principles of History* to the writing of *The New Leviathan*. Notwithstanding, there remain sufficient grounds for believing that among students of history to-day general recognition is accorded to the facts that the particular concern of history is with concrete, unique, and non-recurrent events, to the understanding of which the category of the particular, even the unique, is appropriate; that the subordination of personality to impersonal forces affords no clue to the interpretation of its record; and that the aim of historiography is to present what Collingwood called 'not mere events . . . but actions', an action being 'the unity of the outside and inside of an event', so that 'for history, the object to be discovered is not the mere event but the thought expressed in it'. To the ecclesiastical historian these conclusions are welcome and congenial, and upon them he may venture to construct, and to offer to his fellow-historians an interpretation of the meaning of the process of human history.

For the ecclesiastical historian is made constantly aware that the Christian church, which is the subject of his study, claims to have its origin and foundation in a series of events in the life of its Founder of unique significance for the entire process of history, to which they give meaning and purpose. Likewise his historical canons of study make him bold to claim that the written sources from which his knowledge of this Life is derived bear the authentic character of historical documents, not despite but by reason of their combination of fact and interpretation. From the inspiration of these events wrought *propter nos homines et propter nostram salutem* there springs the historical record of the church, presenting what Figgis called 'the supreme refutation of the impersonal view of history'; and time indeed would fail me to tell of Paul, Constantine, Augustine, Benedict, Francis of Assisi, Luther, Calvin, Loyola, Wesley, and innumerable others who by its illumination have changed and fashioned the course of history. So, like the professor in Browning's *Christmas Eve*, the student of ecclesiastical history must return constantly to these *gesta Dei per Christum* from which the church takes its charter and character; and like him I must needs make this my *apologia* for having thus

> aimed this eve's discourse,
> Since where could be a fitter time
> For tracing backward to its prime
> This Christianity, this lake,
> This reservoir whereat we slake,
> From one or other bank, our thirst?

'From one or other bank'; for the Christian philosophy of history seeks its consummation and fulfilment beyond history, affirming that they truly interpret its purpose who confess themselves to be strangers and pilgrims on the earth, and thereby make it manifest *se patriam inquirere.* As the ecclesiastical historian traces the fortunes of the church militant here in earth, he is made mindful often of the words of Augustine in a famous passage of the *De Civitate Dei*: 'Of Cain it is written that he founded a city; but Abel, being the pattern of a true pilgrim, did

31

not do so. For the commonwealth of saints is not of this world, though it gives birth to citizens in whose persons it performs its pilgrimage, until the time of its kingdom comes, when it will gather them all together in their resurrection-bodies, and when the promised kingdom will be given to them, *ubi cum suo principe rege saeculorum sine ullo temporis fine regnabunt.*'